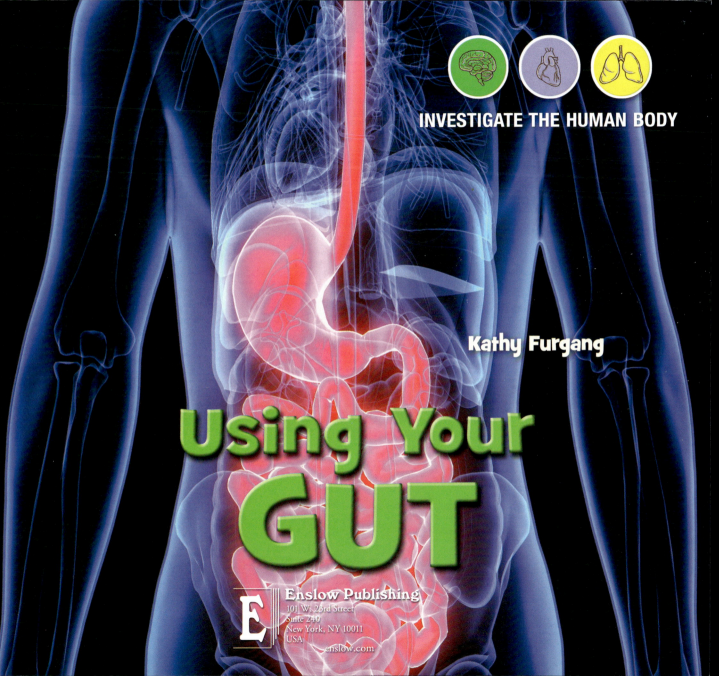

INVESTIGATE THE HUMAN BODY

Kathy Furgang

Using Your GUT

Enslow Publishing
101 W. 23rd Street
Suite 240
New York, NY 10011
USA

enslow.com

••• Words to Know

acid Matter made by the body to break down food.

bacteria Tiny organisms in the body that can be harmful or helpful to our health.

colon The main part of the large intestine. It holds and then passes waste from the body.

digestive system The body system that breaks down food for the body to use for nutrients and energy.

esophagus A soft, muscular tube that moves food down to the stomach.

large intestine The part of the digestive system that food travels through just before it leaves the body.

liver The body organ that helps get rid of unhealthy chemicals in the body.

nutrient A substance that gives the body what it needs to live and grow.

pancreas The body part behind the stomach that provides chemicals that help with digestion.

small intestine The part of the digestive system that food moves to after leaving the stomach.

••• Contents

Food on the Way Down

●●● Have you ever had an upset stomach? You can feel it in your gut. But what is your gut, anyway? Your gut is another word for your **digestive system**. This system breaks down the food you eat. Food gives your body the **nutrients** and energy you need to live and grow. So, your gut is quite an important part of your body.

Starting the Journey

Everything you eat goes on a journey through your body. First, you take in food by chewing and swallowing it. That's just the start. Your gut must do a lot of work before the food can leave your body as waste.

4

Your gut plays a key role in how your body handles the food you eat.

Your gut lets you know when you've had too much to eat.

Growing Belly

The stomach is as small as a tennis ball when it is empty. When it is full, it can expand to the size of a football.

The teeth and tongue work to break down food in your mouth.

Chew and Swallow

Your mouth is the first body part on food's journey through the body. The food you eat is broken into smaller pieces when you chew. Your saliva also wets and mixes the food as you eat. Your teeth and tongue move the food around and toward the back of your throat.

Next, it's time to swallow your food. As muscles squeeze and relax, the food moves down your **esophagus**. The esophagus is a tube that moves the food to your stomach. This is the start of the food's journey through your body.

7

Through the Gut

When food reaches your stomach, it sits there for a while. For about four hours, your stomach hits the food with strong **acids**. These liquids break down the food even more. They also kill harmful **bacteria** that might be in the food you have eaten.

Your muscles shift the food around your stomach. This helps mix the food with digestive juices. At this point, your food is like soup. It gets moved to the next part of your gut—the **small intestine**. Food that enters the stomach looks much different than food that exits!

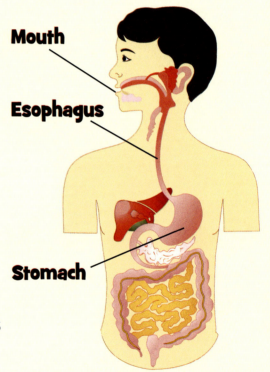

Mouth

Esophagus

Stomach

The stomach adds strong acids to food to break it down.

The Small Intestine

A lot of digestion happens in the small intestine. This organ absorbs, or takes in, the nutrients from foods. Remember those strong acids that were added to the food in your stomach? The small intestine adds liquids that make the acids less harmful to the body. The digested nutrients from the small intestine are absorbed through its walls. The nutrients then get into your blood and move through your body.

It takes from three to six hours for foods to pass through the twists and turns of the small intestine. Food that is not absorbed into the blood during this time moves into the next part of the gut—the **large intestine**.

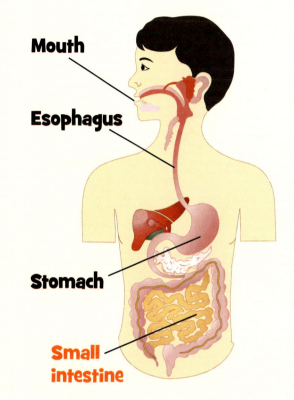

Mouth

Esophagus

Stomach

Small intestine

Most digestion happens in the small intestine. It allows the body to absorb the nutrients in the food you eat.

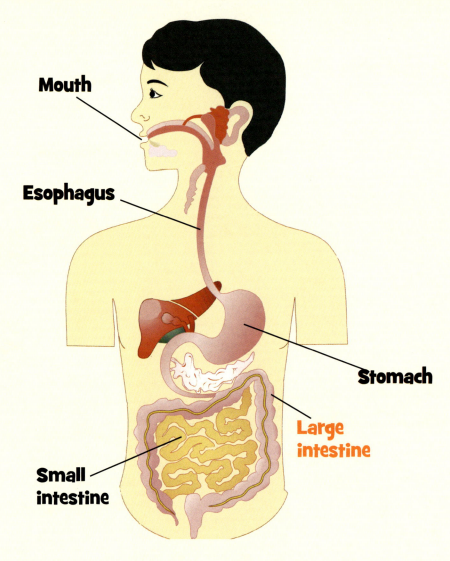

Mouth

Esophagus

Stomach

Large intestine

Small intestine

The large intestine is the last part of food's journey through your body.

Not So Small

If you stretched it from end to end, the small intestine is 21 feet (6.5 meters) long.

The Large Intestine

The large intestine is named for how wide it is. It is about 3 inches (8 centimeters) around. That's much larger than the small intestine, which is just 1 inch (3 cm) around.

The large intestine is 5 feet (1.5 m) long. As materials pass through, liquids are absorbed out of them. As a result, the materials in the large intestine harden. Then they move to the main part of the large intestine, the **colon**. By now, your food is in a much different form than when you first ate it. Your body has taken the nutrients it needs from the food. The food stays in your colon for a day or two until it is ready to exit your body as waste.

Your Gut in Control

Your gut, or digestive system, is more than just the path your food takes. Other organs around your intestines also play an important role. They release chemicals to help you digest food.

The Liver

The **liver** sits just next to the stomach. It breaks down fats from the foods you eat. It removes unhealthy chemicals, called toxins.

The Pancreas

The **pancreas** sits behind the stomach. It releases a chemical that controls the amount of sugar in the blood. Have you ever heard of someone having diabetes? This is a disease that can occur if the pancreas cannot control the amount of sugar in the blood.

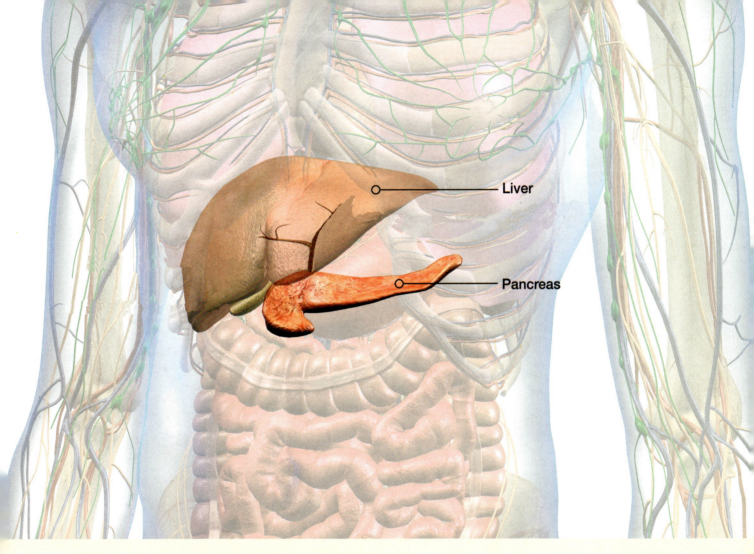

Liver

Pancreas

The liver and the pancreas both help your gut. Bile from the liver helps break down fats, while chemicals from the pancreas aid in digestion.

Matter made by the pancreas
breaks down sugars you eat.

Hard Worker

The liver performs more than 500 jobs for the body. Its main job is to clean the blood. It also makes and stores fuel the body needs to function. A damaged liver can even heal itself over time.

Wasted Away

Some parts of the digestive system are pretty gross, but important,. In order for food to make it all the way through the body, it must be released as waste. That means poop. You may have heard the phrase "bowel movement." That's exactly what happens when waste leaves your body. The bowels hold the waste until muscles move. The movement is what removes the waste from the body.

Drinking liquids such as water helps the body remove waste.

It can take days for your body to totally digest some foods. A person's age and diet affect how long it takes food to be digested. The body digests fruits and vegetables faster than most meats.

Treat Your Gut Right

When your gut is working as it should, you feel great. When it is feeling bad, there are things you can do to help. It's important to keep your gut working right!

Food for Thought

Eating right is the most important part of having a healthy gut. A mix of fruits and vegetables helps keep the digestive system strong. Limit fatty foods in your diet. They slow down digestion. Eat as many fresh foods as you can. Packaged foods made in factories have a lot of added salt and sugar. They may also have other added ingredients that are not healthy for your gut.

Eating lots of fruits and vegetables helps keep your gut working well.

Get Moving

Staying active helps the digestive system work correctly. Moving your body helps keep food moving through it.

Bacteria: Good and Bad

You may think of bacteria as something that makes you sick. But there are good and bad bacteria. Your stomach and intestines are lined with good bacteria that keep you healthy. But, your gut bacteria sometimes need some help. Keeping a healthy diet can keep the bacteria in your body balanced. Foods like yogurt have good bacteria in them that will keep your gut working well.

Adding to the healthy bacteria in your gut can keep you healthy.

Healthy Gut, Healthy Body

From the moment food enters your body to the moment it leaves, your gut is hard at work. Your intestines break down and digest food. Nutrients pump through your blood to give you energy. Your body gets rid of what it does not need or cannot use. Help keep your gut healthy and strong with the things you eat and do!

Activity: Keep a Gut Checklist

●●● Keep track of your gut-healthy activities for three days.

1. Write down the foods and activities you do for three days. Also, write how many glasses of water you drink. Only count water—no other drinks.

2. Write about how you feel, especially after you eat or exercise. How can you improve your activities to improve how you feel?

3. Try to make the change you identified. Then keep track of your gut-healthy activities for the next three days.

Gut Checklist

	FOOD	ACTIVITY	WATER
DAY 1			
DAY 2			
DAY 3			

Keep track of your gut-healthy activities for three days.

Learn More

Books

Dorling Kindersley. *Are You What You Eat?* London, UK: Dorling Kindersley, 2015.

Manolis, Kay. *The Digestive System*. Minnetonka, MN: Bellwether Media, 2016.

Simon, Seymour. *Guts: All About Our Digestive System*. New York, NY: HarperCollins, 2019.

Websites

Choose MyPlate for Kids
www.choosemyplate.gov/kids
This website includes information for children about a healthy diet, as well as games, activity sheets, videos, and songs.

Health Powered Kids
healthpoweredkids.org/
Find activities to help you make good choices about health, eating, and exercise.

Kids Health
kidshealth.org/en/kids/?WT.ac=p2k
Play games and take quizzes about health and the human body.

Index

Published in 2020 by Enslow Publishing, LLC
101 W. 23rd Street, Suite 240, New York, NY 10011

Library of Congress Cataloging-in-Publication Data

Names: Furgang, Kathy, author.

Title: Using your gut / Kathy Furgang.

Description: New York : Enslow Publishing, 2020. | Series: Investigate the human body | Audience: Grade K-4. | Includes bibliographical references and index.

Identifiers: LCCN 2019008258| ISBN 9781978512955 (library bound) | ISBN 9781978512931 (paperback) | ISBN 9781978512948 (6 pack)

Subjects: LCSH: Digestive organs--Juvenile literature. | Gastrointestinal system--Juvenile literature.

Classification: LCC QM301 .F87 2020 | DDC 612.3--dc23

LC record available at https://lccn.loc.gov/2019008258

Printed in the United States of America

Photos Credits: Using Your Gut – Research by Bruce Donnola
Cover, p. 1 Life science/Shutterstock.com; pp. 3, 7 Jose Luis Pelaez/The Image Bank; pp. 3, 8, 9, 10 snapgalleria/iStock/Getty Images; pp. 3, 14 hartcreations/E+/Getty Images; pp. 3, 20 © iStockphoto.com/carebott; pp. 3, 23 Victor Brave/Shutterstock.com; p. 5, 18 Monkey Business Images/Shutterstock.com; p. 6 Standret/Shutterstock.com; p. 13 © iStockphoto.com/Hank Grebe; p. 16 wonderlandstock/Alamy Stock Photo; cover graphics blackpencil/Shutterstock.com.